THE TEACHING OF HISTORY

THE TEACHING OF HISTORY

Ernest C. Hartwell, M.A.

Superintendent of Schools,
Petoskey,
Mich.

MJP Publishers

Chennai   New Delhi   Tirunelveli

ISBN 978-81-8094-244-0 **MJP Publishers**

All rights reserved
Printed and bound in India

No. 44 Nallathambi Street,
Triplicane,
Chennai 600 005

MJP 221   © Publishers, 2016

Publisher : C.Janarthanan

CONTENTS

EDITOR'S INTRODUCTION

This volume is offered as a guide to history teachers of the high school and the upper grammar grades. It is directly concerned with the teaching methods to be employed in the history period. The author assumes the limiting conditions that surround classroom instruction of the present day; he also takes for granted the teacher's sympathy with modern aims in history instruction. All discussions of purpose and content are therefore subordinated to a clear presentation of the details of effective teaching technique.

The reader into whose hands this volume falls will be deeply interested in the ideals of teaching implied in the concrete suggestions given in the following pages, for after all the value of any system of special methods rests, not merely on its apparent and immediate psychological effectiveness, but also on the social purposes which it is devised to serve. It must be recognized at the outset that history has a social purpose. However much university teaching may be interested in truth for its own sake, an interest necessarily basic to the service of all other ends, the teaching of the lower public schools must take into account the relevancy of historical fact to current and future problems which concern men and women engaged in the common social life. So the elementary and secondary school teachers of the more progressive sort recognize that the way in which historical truths are selected and related to one another determines two things:

1.   Whether our group experiences as interpreted in history will have any intelligent effect upon men's appreciations of current social difficulties, and

2.   Whether history will make a more vital appeal to youth at school.

Certainly children, whose interests arise not alone from their innate impulses, but also from the world in which they have lived from the beginning, will be eager to know the past that is of dominant concern to the present. It is clear gain in the psychology of instruction if history is a socially live thing. The children will be more eager to acquire knowledge; they will hold it longer, because it is significant; and they will keep it fresh after school days are over because life will recall and review pertinent knowledge again and again. There can be no separation between the dominant social interests of community life and effective pedagogical procedure; the former in large part determines the latter.

Such educational reforms in history teaching as have already won acceptance confirm the existence of this vital relation between current social interests and the learning process. The barren learning of names and dates has long since been supplanted by a study of sequences among events. The technical details of wars and political administrations have given way to a study of wide economic and social movements in which battles and laws are merely overt results reinforcing the current of change. History, once a self-inclosed school discipline, has undergone an intellectual expansion which takes into account all the aspects of life which influence it, making geographical, economic, and biographical materials its aids. All these and many other minor changes attest the fact that a vital mode of instruction always tends to accompany that view of history which regards the study of the past as a revelation of real social life.

The author's suggestions will, therefore, be of distinct value to at least two groups of history teachers. Those who believe in the larger uses of history teaching, so much argued of late, will find here the procedures that will express the ideals and obtain the results they seek. Those who are not yet ready to accept modern doctrine, but who feel a keen discontent with the older procedure, will find in these pages many suggestions that will appeal to them as worthy of experimental use. It may be that the successful use of many methods here suggested may be the easy way for them to come into an acceptance of the larger principles of current educational reform.

THE TEACHING OF HISTORY

I

SOME PRELIMINARY CONSIDERATIONS

Assumptions as to the teacher of history

This monograph will make no attempt to analyze the personality of the ideal teacher. It is assumed that the teacher of history has an adequate preparation to teach his subject, that he is in good health, and that his usefulness is unimpaired by discontent with his work or cynicism about the world. It is presupposed that he understands the wisdom of correlating in his instruction the geography, social progress, and economic development of the people which his class are studying. He is aware that the pupil should experience something more than a kaleidoscopic view of isolated facts. He recognizes the folly of requiring four years of high school English for the purpose of cultivating clear, fluent, and accurate expression, only to relax the effort when the student comes into the history class. He knows that the precision, logic, and habit of definite thinking exacted by the pursuit of the scientific subjects should not be laid aside when the student attempts to trace the rise of nations. Let us go so far as to assume a teacher who is both pedagogical and practical; scholarly without being musty; imbued with a love for his subject and yet familiar with actual human experience.

Actual conditions confronted by the teacher

There are from one hundred and eighty to two hundred recitation periods of forty-five minutes each, minus the holidays, opening exercises, athletic mass meetings, and other respites, in which to teach a thousand years of ancient history, twenty centuries of English history, or the story of our own people. The age of the student will be from thirteen to eighteen. His judgment is immature; his knowledge of books, small; his interest, far from zealous. He will have three other subjects to prepare and his time is limited. Also, he is a citizen of the Republic and by his vote will shortly influence, for good or ill, the destinies of the nation.

The purpose of this monograph is to discuss the means by which the teacher can engender in this student a genuine enthusiasm for the subject, stimulate research and historical judgment, correlate history, geography, literature, and the arts, cultivate proper ideals of government, establish a habit of systematic note-taking, and possibly prepare the student for college entrance examinations.

II

HOW TO BEGIN THE COURSE

Very obviously each moment of the child's time and preparation should be wisely directed. Each recitation should perform its full measure of usefulness, in testing, drilling, and teaching. There will be no time for valueless note-taking, duplication of map-book work, ambiguous or foolish questioning, aimless argument, or junketing excursions.

What should be done on the day of enrollment

The day that the child enrolls in class should begin his assigned work. In the first ten minutes of the first meeting of the class, while the teacher is collecting the enrollment cards, he should also gather some data as to his students' previous work in history. This information will be of considerable assistance to the teacher in letting him know what he may reasonably expect of his new pupils. The class should not depart without a definite assignment for the next day. Let the preparation for the first recitation consist in answering such questions as:—

1. What is the name of the text you are to use? (Know its precise title.)

2. What is the name, reputation, and position of the author?

3. Of what other books is he the author?

4. Read the preface of the book.

5. What do you think are the purposes of the subject you are about to take up?

6. Give the titles and authors of other books on the same period of history.

7. What has been your method of study in other courses of history?

What should be done at the first meeting of the class

On the second day when the class assembles, let as many of the students as possible be sent to the board to answer questions on the day's assignment. The pupil will immediately discover that the teacher purposes to hold the class strictly responsible for the preparation of assigned work. The teacher will face a class prepared to ask intelligent questions about the course they are entering upon. The class will discover that work is to begin at once. The inertia of the vacation will be immediately overcome.

Necessity for definite instruction in methods of preparing a lesson

Having secured, by class discussion and the work at the board, satisfactory answers to the first six questions, and having assigned the lesson for the next day, the remainder of the hour and, if necessary, the rest of the week should be spent in outlining for the student a method of study. That very few students of high school age possess habits of systematic study, needs no discussion. In spite of all that their grade teachers may have done for them, their tendency is to pass over unfamiliar words, allusions, and expressions, without troubling to use a dictionary. The average high school student will not read the fine print at the bottom of the page, or use a map for the location of places mentioned in the text without special instruction to do so. He will set himself no unassigned tasks in memory work. It is the first business of the good instructor to teach the student *how* to study. The first step in this process is to impress on the student's mind that systematic preparation in the history class is as necessary as in Latin, physics, or geometry. Then let the following or similar instructions be given him:—

1. Provide yourself with an envelope of small cards or pieces of note paper. Label each with the subject of the lesson and the date of its preparation. These envelopes should be always at hand during your study and preparation. They should be preserved and filed from day to day.

2. Read the lesson assigned for the day in the textbook, including all notes and fine print.

3. Write on a sheet of note paper all the unfamiliar words, allusions, or expressions. Later, look these up in the dictionary or other reference.

4. Record the dates which you think worthy to be remembered.

5. Discover and make a note of all the apparent contradictions, inconsistencies, or inaccuracies in the author's statements.

6. Use the map for all the places mentioned in the lesson. Be able to locate them when you come to class.

7. In nearly every text there is a list of books for library use, given at the beginning or end of each chapter. Make yourself familiar with this bibliography.

8. Read the special questions assigned for the day by the teacher.

9. Go to the library. If the book for which you are in search is not to be found, try another.

10. Learn to use an index. If the topic for which you are looking does not appear in the index, try looking for the same thing under another name; or under some related topic.

11. Having found the material in one book, use more than one if your time permits. When you feel that you have secured the material which will make a complete answer to the question, *write the answer on one of your cards for keeping notes.*

12. Remember that the teacher will ask constantly *what* was done, *when* was it done, and, most

important of all, *why* it was done. Make a list of the questions which you think most likely to be asked on the lesson and ascertain whether you can answer them without the use of your notes or text.

13. If possible practice your answers aloud. It will make you the more ready when called on in class.

14. Keep a list of things which are not clear to you and about which you wish to ask questions.

15. Before completing your preparation, read over these instructions and be sure that you have complied with them.

It may be claimed that no high school student can be expected to follow such instructions and that to secure such a daily preparation is impossible; in answer to which it must be admitted that merely a perfunctory talk on methods of preparation will accomplish little. If the instruction just suggested is to bear fruit, the teacher must take pains to see that it is followed. Carefully to prepare his lesson according to a definite plan must become a *habit* with the student. Facility, accuracy, and thoroughness are impossible otherwise. Haphazard methods are wasteful of time and unproductive of results. The teacher can afford to emphasize method during the first few weeks of the course. The time thus spent in assisting the pupil to develop definite habits of study will pay rich dividends for the remainder of the student's life. Daily inquiry as to the method of study pursued, frequent examination of the student's notes, questions on the important dates selected, the books used for preparation, new words discovered, and so on, will keep the importance of the plan before the class and do much to foster the habit of systematic preparation.

The question of note-taking

On the question of notebook work, there will always be a considerable difference of opinion. It is much easier to state what notebook work should not be than to outline precisely how it should be conducted. Certainly it should not be overdone. It should not be an exercise usurping time disproportionate to its value. It should not be required primarily for exhibition purposes, although such notes as are kept should be kept neatly and spelled correctly.

Students should be encouraged to keep their envelope of note paper always at hand during recitation and while reading. The habit of jotting down facts, opinions, statistics, comparisons, and contradictions *while they are being read* is most desirable and worthy of cultivation. The student should be taught the wisdom of keeping his notes in a neat, legible, and easily available form. Shorthand methods should be discouraged. With a little tactful direction early in the year, the student may be led to form a most useful habit. The greater the proportion of intelligent note-taking that is done without compulsion, the better. No more notes should be *required* than the teacher can honestly look over, correct, and grade. It is better to require no notes at all than to accept careless, superficial inaccuracies as honest work. One curse of high school history teaching is the tendency of young teachers trained in college history classes to assign more work than the student can honestly do or the teacher properly correct.

As has already been intimated, history notes should not be kept in a book. The required notes should be kept on separate sheets of paper. The topics should be clearly indicated at the top of each sheet. The authorities used in arriving at the answer should always be given, with the volume, chapter, and page. The notes on related topics should be put into an envelope and properly labeled. After the recitation the student can make any necessary corrections in his notes without spoiling their appearance. He will simply substitute a new sheet for the old. If the teacher discovers in his periodic examination of the notes that some of the matter asked for has not been properly covered or that errors have not been corrected, the notes needing revision can be detained for use in a conference with the student, while the others are returned. If at any time after completing his high school work the student desires to use the data contained in his notes or to add to them matter which he may later read, they are in available form. For convenience and neatness, for present use, and future reference this device is far superior to the formal notebook. It has the further advantage of accustoming the student to the method of note-taking which will be required of those who go to college.

It would save much valuable time, at present frequently wasted in writing useless notes, if the teacher constantly squared his notebook requirements with questions such as these:—

1.   Is the notebook work as I am conducting it calculated to develop the habit of critical reading?

2.   Does the time spent in writing up notes justify itself by fixing in the child's mind new and really relevant information not given in the text?

3.   Is it teaching students to combine facts, opinions, and statistics, to form conclusions really their own?

4.   Is the amount of work required reasonable when it is remembered that the child has three other subjects to prepare, that he is from thirteen to eighteen years of age, and more or less unfamiliar with a library?

5.   Am I able carefully and punctually to correct all the notes required?

Whatever the method the teacher thinks best to be used should be explained early in the course and thereafter the student should be held scrupulously responsible for such requirements as are made.

Instruction in the use of the library and indexes

Having discussed with the class the questions assigned on the day of enrollment and explained the method of study recommended for their use, it will be well for the teacher to devote some time to instruction in the use of the library. It is possible that the older classes will require very little of this, but there are few classes where an hour, at least, cannot well be spent in a discussion of indexes, titles, and relative value of the works on various subjects. This hour need not be the regular recitation period. A session before or after school could be devoted to the purpose. The teacher's instruction, however, will be greatly assisted if the students are asked to prepare answers before coming to class to such questions as the following:—

1. How much previous work have you done in the library?

2. Of what use do you think the library should be to you in the course you are just entering?

3. What is a source book? Of what use are source books?

4. What source books on this period of history are in the library?

5. What do you think will be the best references for questions on the artistic, industrial, political, social, economic, and military phases of the history you are about to study?

6. What encyclopedias and works of general reference are in your library?

The preparation of answers to such questions as these will present to the student some of the difficulties inevitable to his future library work and will send him to class prepared to ask intelligent questions. It will enable the teacher accurately to gauge how much his students already know about a library and its uses.

The value and advantage of library work should be carefully explained to the class. It is a great error to allow pupils to think of their library work as drudgery, assigned solely to keep them busy or to make the course difficult. There are too few boys to-day with a genuine love of books, partly no doubt due to the fact that a reference library has become for them, not a rich mine of interesting matter, but a hydra-headed interrogation point. A great good has been done the student who has been taught the pleasure of using books. Nor is such a thing impossible. Nothing gives greater satisfaction to the normal high school boy than to find an error in the text, the teacher's statements, or the map. He takes pleasure in confuting the statistics or judgments quoted in class, by others of opposite trend, encountered in his reading. He enjoys asking keen questions. If the student is told that the library work is for the purpose of cultivating his powers of investigation and adding to the matter in the text many interesting details; if the library requirements are reasonable and wisely directed; if he is given an opportunity to *use* the information he has gathered from his reading, his interest in books will steadily increase.

The teacher should explain the value of remembering accurately the titles and the authors of books used for reference. The silly habit of referring to an authority as "the book bound in green" or "the large book by what's his name" is easily prevented if taken in time.

The teacher should discover by assignments made in class what degree of proficiency in the use of an index is already possessed by his pupils. There are few classes where the use of an index is thoroughly understood. Time should be taken to demonstrate the quickest possible methods of finding what a book contains. The use of the catalogue and card index should be carefully explained and illustrated.

Attention should be called to the best sources on the various phases of the history to be studied. There ought to be no poor histories in the library, but if there are any to which the students have access, warning should be given against their use.

The value of periodicals and current literature for work in history should be illustrated and the use of *Poole's Index* and the *Readers Guide* explained.

The class should be acquainted with the rules of the library and cautioned against the misuse of books. The necessity of leaving reference books where all the class can use them should be made apparent.

Direction in the use of the library, like instruction in the method of study, is a prerequisite to the best results in high school history classes, for no matter how conscientious the teacher, the recitation will be deadly if the student has no working knowledge of the library nor proper method of preparation. A class unable to ask intelligent questions about the work is not ready for the presentation of additional matter by the teacher. It is no difficult matter for a teacher to entertain his class for an hour with interesting incidents of the period in which the lesson occurs. A history teacher who cannot talk interestingly for an hour on any of the great periods of history has surely missed his calling. But to keep a class quiet, to retain their attention, to amuse and entertain, is far from making history vital. If the recitation is to be really vital, the students must do most of the talking, the criticizing, and the questioning. There can be none of these worth while without proper preparation.

III

THE ASSIGNMENT OF THE LESSON

Careful assignment will reveal to the student the relation of geography and history

The recitation can never hope to achieve its maximum helpfulness unless the lesson be intelligently assigned. The work required must be reasonable in amount, and not so exacting as to discourage interest. Daily direction to look up unfamiliar words, expressions, and allusions must be given until the habit becomes fixed. Warning against possible geographical misconceptions should be given when necessary, together with directions to use the map for places, routes, and boundaries. A few questions asked in advance, with the purpose of bringing out the relation of the geography to the history in the lesson, will be of great assistance. For example, if the class are to study the Louisiana Purchase, the full significance of that revolutionary event will be made much clearer if the student is asked to prepare answers before coming to class to such questions as the following:—

1. What States are included in the purchase?

2. What is its area? How does it compare with the area of the original thirteen States?

3. What geographical reasons caused Napoleon to sell it?

4. What influence did the purchase have on our retention of the territory east of the Mississippi? Why?

5. How many people live to-day in the territory included in the purchase?

His power of analysis and criticism will be stimulated

A lesson should be so assigned that the student will read the text with his eye critically open to inconsistencies, contradictions, and inaccuracies. With a text of six hundred pages, and with a hundred and eighty recitations in which to cover them, it is not too much to expect that the average of three or four pages daily shall be studied so thoroughly that the student can analyze and summarize each day's lesson. The teacher should not make such analysis in advance of the recitation, but he should so assign the lesson that the student will be prepared to give one when he comes to class. A word in advance by the teacher will prompt the student who is studying the American Revolution, to classify its causes as direct and indirect, economic and political, social and religious. There is no difficulty in finding good authorities who disagree as to the effect on America of the English trade restrictions. Callendar's *Economic History of the United States* quotes five of the best authorities on this point, and covers the case in a few pages. A reference by the teacher to this or some other authority will bring out a lively discussion on the justice of the American resistance. Let the class be asked to account for the colonial opposition to the

Townshend Acts, when the Stamp Act Congress had declared that the regulation of the Colonies' external trade was properly within the powers of Parliament. Let the class be asked to explain a statement that the Declaration of Independence does not mention the real underlying causes of the Revolution. A few suggestions and advanced questions of this sort will stimulate a critical analysis of the statements in the text, and send the student to class keen for an intelligent discussion.

Ordinarily, when a class is averaging three or four pages of the text daily, it is an error for the teacher to point out in advance certain dates and statistics that need not be memorized. Such selection should be left to the student. During the recitation the teacher will discover what dates, statistics, and other matter the student has selected as worthy to be memorized, and if correction is necessary it may then be made. It dulls the edge of the pupil's enthusiasm to be told in advance that some of the text is not worthy to be remembered. Furthermore such instruction does nothing to develop the student's sense of historical proportion, for it substitutes the judgment of the teacher for that of the pupil.

Advance questions asking explanation of statements made in the text, or by other authors dealing with the same period, insure that the lesson will be read understandingly and that the author's statements will be carefully analyzed. Such declarations as the following are illustrations of statements whose explanation might profitably be required in advance:—

1.   "The Constitution was extracted by necessity from a reluctant people."

2.   "Oregon was a make-weight for Texas."

3.   "The greatest evil of slavery was that it prevented the South from accumulating capital."

4.   "The day that France possesses New Orleans we must marry ourselves to the British fleet."

5.   "The cause of free labor won a substantial triumph in the Missouri Compromise."

6.   "The second war with England was not one of necessity, policy, or interest on the part of the Americans; it was rather one of party prejudice and passion."

The conditions in other countries will add to his comprehension of the facts in the lesson

In so far as the next lesson requires an understanding of the history or conditions of another country, the attention of the class should be directed in advance to such necessity. Special references or brief reports may be advisable. A few well-selected advance questions will send the class to recitation prepared to discuss what otherwise the teacher must explain. A few questions on the character of James II, his ideals of government, the chief causes of the revolution of 1688, and its most important results will do much to explain the colonial resistance to Andros. A few questions designed to bring out the imperative necessity of English resistance to Napoleon will make clear the hostile commercial decrees, impressment, and interference with the rights of neutral ships. Such questions reduce the necessity of explanation by the teacher to a minimum.

His disposition to study intensively will be encouraged

If the teacher expects the class to deal more intensively than the text with the matters discussed in the lesson, a few advance questions will be of great assistance. Suppose, for example, that the text contents itself with saying that for political reasons the first United States Bank was not rechartered, and shortly after informs the reader that the second United States Bank was rechartered because the State banks had suspended specie payments. The student may or may not be curious about the failure of the first bank to receive a new charter, the operation of State banks, or why they suspended payment in 1814. If he has been properly taught, he probably will be, but if the teacher wishes to discuss these considerations in detail at the next recitation it will be infinitely better to have the facts contributed by the class than for the teacher to do the reciting. It is quite possible that the individual answers to advance questions assigned with such a purpose will be incomplete, but the interest of the class will be incalculably greater if they themselves furnish the bulk of the additional matter required. Collectively the class will usually secure complete answers to reasonable questions. The teacher has his opportunity in supplying such important facts as the students fail to find.

Until the student may reasonably be expected to know the books of the library having to do with his subject, the teacher in giving out an advance lesson should mention by author and title the books most helpful in the preparation of assigned questions; otherwise the student in a perfectly sincere effort to do the work assigned may spend an hour in search of the proper book.

It may be urged that this search is a valuable experience, but it is obviously too costly. As the year advances and the pupil learns more and more about the uses of books and methods of investigation increasingly less specific instruction as to sources should be given by the teacher. Early in the year, with four lessons to prepare daily, the pupil cannot afford an hour simply to search for a book. He needs that hour for preparation of other work, and if by some fortunate conjunction of circumstances his other work is not sufficiently exacting to require it, he cannot hope to appear in history class with a well-prepared lesson if an hour of his time has been spent in simply looking for a book.

It is frequently worth while to spend a few minutes of the recitation in characterizing the epoch in which the events of the lesson take place or in listening to a brief character sketch of the men contributing to these events. Care should of course be taken that biography does not usurp the place of history, but it materially adds to the interest of the recitation if the kings, generals, and statesmen cease to be merely historical characters and become human beings.

His acquaintance with the great men and women of history will be vitalized

It is needless to say that characterizations of men or epochs should not be assigned without instruction as to how they should be prepared. In the case of a great historical character, what is needed for class purposes is not a biography with the dry facts of birth, marriage, death, etc. The report should be brief, but bristling with adjectives supported in each case by at least one fact of the man's life. These may be selected from his personal appearance, private life, amusements, education, obstacles overcome, public services, political sagacity, or military prowess. The sketch may close with a few brief estimates by biographers or historians of his proper place in history.

If a characterization of a period of history is to be required, the teacher should explain that such a characterization should be an exercise in the selection of brief statements of fact reflecting the ideals, institutions, and conditions of the period being described. From histories, source books, fiction, and literature, let the student select facts illustrating such things as the spirit of the laws, conditions at court, public education, amusements of the people, social progress, position of religion, etc. A little time spent in characterizing a period of history and a few of its great men will assist in changing the recital of the bare facts given in the text to an intelligent understanding of conditions and a vital discussion of events. For instance, the ordinary high school text, in dealing with the French and Indian war, speaks briefly of the lack of English success during the early part of the struggle and then says that with the coming of Pitt to the ministry the whole course of events was changed because of the great statesman's wonderful personality. The teacher who wishes to make such a dramatic circumstance really vital to his class must have more information with which to work. A picture of the coarse, vulgar England with its incompetent army and navy, apathetic church, and corrupt government, followed by a stirring character sketch of the great Pitt, will cost but a few minutes of the recitation and will metamorphose a moribund attention to a vital interest.

Care should be taken that the characterizations given in class be properly prepared. To this end it will be well to assign the preparation of these sketches at least a week in advance, at the same time arranging a conference with the student a day or two before the recitation. In this conference the teacher should make such corrections in the pupil's method of preparation and selection of matter as seem necessary. The characterizations should not be read, but delivered by the student facing the class, precisely for the moment as though he were the teacher. Future tests and examinations should hold the class responsible for the facts thus presented. If, as is too often the case in work of this sort, the student giving the report is the sole beneficiary of the exercise, the time required is disproportionate to the benefit derived.

He will correlate the past and the present

If there are facts recounted in the lesson that may be clinched in the student's mind by showing the relation of those facts to present-day conditions or institutions, a few advance questions calculated to bring out this relationship may well be assigned.

It is generally conceded that one chief purpose of history instruction is to enable us to interpret the present and the future in the light of the past, but it all too often happens that current history is forgotten in the recital of facts that are centuries old. Candidates for teachers' certificates in their examinations in United States history show far less knowledge about the great problems and events of the present day than they do of colonial history. The student in English history in our high schools to-day knows all about the Domesday Book, but almost nothing of the recent history of England. Quite possibly the text has nothing to say about it, and it is equally likely that the class may fail to cover the text and miss the little that is actually given. No opportunity should be missed to indicate the bearing of the past on present-day conditions. Even if the events of the lesson exert no direct influence on affairs to-day, their significance may be brought home to the student by an illustration from current history. The account of the Black Death gives excellent occasion for a brief discussion of modern sanitation and the war on the White Plague. The efforts of Parliament to fix wages can be illustrated by some of the minimum wage laws passed by recent legislatures. John Ball's teachings suggest a brief discussion of modern socialism, daily becoming more active in its influence. The medieval trade guilds and modern labor unions; the monopolies of Elizabeth's time and the anti-trust law of to-day; George the Third's two hundred capital crimes and modern methods of penology; the jealousy of Athens in guarding the privilege of citizenship and the facility with which immigrants at present become American citizens are only a few illustrations, indicating the ease with which the past and the present may be correlated.

He will be required to memorize a limited amount of matter verbatim

In assigning a lesson it is sometimes desirable to require certain matter to be learned *verbatim*. In American history the Preamble to the Constitution, the principles of government contained in the Declaration of Independence, the essential doctrine in the Virginia and Kentucky Resolutions, certain clauses of the Constitution, and extracts from other historical documents may well be required to be memorized accurately. It is scarcely to be supposed that the student can improve on the clarity and definiteness of the English in such documents. He is expected to understand the principles which they assert. He may well be required to train his memory to accuracy by learning certain assignments *verbatim*. If memory work received a little more attention in our high schools to-day, we should be less likely to hear the statement of a political creed neutralized by the omission of an important word. We should be less likely to see the classic words of Lincoln mangled beyond recognition by messy misquotation.

The assignment of advance questions such as have been suggested possesses several advantages. It makes it possible for the teacher to hold the class responsible for definite preparation, very much as the teacher in algebra is able to do with the problems assigned in advance. It forces the students to do most of the talking. It encourages an intelligent use of the library in a manner calculated to develop the student's powers of investigation. If the pupil forgets most of his history, but retains the ability to investigate carefully, thoroughly, and critically, the plan has more than justified itself. The plan enables the teacher to spend his time in explanation of what the pupil has been unable to do for herself, and thus effects a considerable saving in time. It would be interesting to secure a statement of how much of the teacher's time is ordinarily spent in doing for the student in recitation what he should have done for himself before coming to class. It substitutes for the pupil's snap judgment, given without much thought and too frequently influenced by the inflection of the teacher's voice, an opinion that has resulted from research and deliberation unbiased by the teacher's personal views.

It is too much to expect high school pupils to solve historical problems extemporaneously. If inferences and contrasts other than those given in the text are to be drawn, if statements are to be defended or opposed, the high school student should be given time to prepare his answer. Aside from the injustice of any other procedure, it is a hopeless waste of time to spend the precious minutes of the recitation in gathering negative replies and worthless judgments.

Methods of preparing questions assigned in advance

It may be urged that such an assignment of a lesson as that proposed is too ambitious and that it exacts too much of the teacher's time. In answer it should be said that specialists in history ought surely to have read widely enough and studied deeply enough to be *able* to select intelligent questions of the sort suggested. We have assumed that the teacher has made adequate preparation for his work. Certainly, then, he should be ready to explain the social, geographical, and economic relation of the events mentioned in the lesson. He should know their bearing on current history. He should always have ready a fund of information, additional to that given in the text. In preparing advance questions for distribution to the class the teacher is preparing his own lesson. He may be doing it a day or two earlier than he would otherwise do, but surely he is performing no labor additional to what may reasonably be expected of him. As to the time required to prepare copies of the questions for distribution when the class convenes, it may be said that a neostyle or mimeograph, with which all large schools and many small ones are equipped, makes short work of preparing as many copies of the questions as desired. If there is a commercial department in connection with the school, an available stenographer, or a willing student helper, the teacher may easily relieve himself of the work of supplying the copies. If none of these expedients are possible, it is no Herculean task to write each day on the board the few questions for the next lesson. It will entail no great loss of time if the class are asked to copy them when they first come to recitation. If it is possible to copy them after the recitation, so much the better. And beyond the obvious advantages of a carefully assigned lesson it must be remembered that in the assignment of special topics, in private conferences with the student, in the correction of notes, in giving assistance in the library, the teacher has an opportunity to cultivate a sympathetic relation between himself and the class of inestimable service in securing the best results.

IV

THE METHOD OF THE RECITATION

Assumptions as to the recitation room

Let us now assume that the recitation will be held in a quiet room free from the distracting influence of poor light, poor ventilation, and inadequate seating capacity. The blackboard space is ample for the whole class, the erasers and chalk are at hand, the maps, charts, and globe are where they can be used without stumbling over them. The teacher can give his whole attention to the class. Discipline should take care of itself. The pupil who is interested will not be seriously out of order.

What the teacher should aim to accomplish

The problem, then, is so to expend the forty-five minutes in which the teacher and class are together that:—

1. So far as possible the atmosphere and setting of the period being studied may be reproduced.

2. The great historical characters spoken of in the lesson may become for the student real men and women with whom he will afterwards feel a personal acquaintance.

3. The events described will be understood and properly interpreted in their relation to geography, and the economic and social progress of the world.

4. Causes and effects shall be properly analyzed.

5. And that there shall be left sufficient time for the occasional review necessary to any good instruction.

Work at the blackboard

The first five minutes may profitably be spent at the board, each member of the class being asked to write a complete answer to one of the assigned questions. Whatever may happen later in the recitation each student has had at least this much of an opportunity for self-expression, and his work should be neat, workmanlike, complete, and accurate. By this device the alert teacher will secure in the first five minutes of the recitation hour a fairly accurate idea of each student's preparation, the weak spots in his understanding of the lesson, and the errors to be corrected. He may even be able to record a grade for the work done.

Special reports

The class having taken their seats, the next order of business should be the reports on special topics assigned for the purpose of making the period of history under discussion more interesting and vital. As has been said, these reports should not be read, but delivered by the pupil facing the class. The class should be encouraged to ask questions on the report when finished and the student responsible for the report should be expected to answer any reasonable inquiry. If other students are able to contribute to the topics reported on, they should be encouraged to do so. Let the teacher be sure that he has sounded the depths of the students' information and curiosity before he himself discusses the report. If the device of reports delivered in class is to justify itself, the matter contained in them must be so arranged and discussed that the whole class receives real benefit. The ingenious teacher will be able to establish a tradition in his course for a careful preparation and critical discussion of these reports. The rivalry of students for excellence in this work is not difficult to stimulate. A premium should be put on criticism which finds mentioned in the characterization qualities inconsistent with the facts recorded in the text, or omissions which the facts of the text seem to justify.

Fundamental principles of good questioning

It is not likely that the teacher will find it advisable to require reports at every recitation nor that the reports and their discussion will consume, at the most, longer than ten or fifteen minutes of any class period. There must always be time for direct oral questioning on the facts of the lesson; questioning that will test the student's memory, ability to analyze, and powers of expression. Certain principles are fundamental to good questioning in any recitation.

1. The questions should be brief.

2. They should be prepared by the teacher before coming to recitation. This will insure rapidity. A vast deal of time is lost by the unfortunate habit possessed by many teachers of never having the next question ready to use.

3. They should precede the name of the pupil required to answer it.

4. They should not be leading questions to which the pupil can guess the answers.

5. They should be grammatically stated with but one possible interpretation.

6. Except for purposes of rapid review they should not be answerable with yes or no.

7. They should be asked in a voice loud enough to be heard by all the class, and only once.

8. They should be asked in no regular order, but nevertheless in such a way that every member of the class will have a chance to recite.

Some additional suggestions for teachers of history

There are additional suggestions particularly applicable to the teacher of history.

1. In all the questioning remember the purposes of the recitation. Ask questions knowing exactly what you wish as an answer. There is no time for aimless or idle questioning.

2. Inquire frequently as to the books used in preparation of the lesson. Let no allusion or statement in the text go unexplained. Let none of the author's conclusions or opinions go unchallenged. Ask the student for inconsistencies, inaccuracies, or contradictions in the text. Put a premium on their discovery. Insist on the student's authority for statements other than those given in the text.

3. Do not use the heavy-typed words frequently found at the head of the paragraph or the topical heads furnished by the text, if it can be avoided. The pupil should not be allowed to remember his history by its location in the text.

4. Be sure that the class have an opportunity to recite on the questions assigned for their advance preparation. Nothing is more discouraging to a student than carefully to prepare the work required and then fail of an opportunity either to recite upon or to discuss it.

5. Discover the tastes, shortcomings, and abilities of your individual students and direct your future questions accordingly. There will usually be in the class the boy who is glib without being accurate. He should be questioned on definite facts. There will be the student whose analysis of events is good, but whose powers of description are poor. Adapt your questions to his special need. There will be the pupil with the tendency to memorize the text *verbatim*. There will be the student who knows the facts of the lesson, but who fails to

remember the sequence of events—the kind who never can tell whether the Exclusion Bill came before or after the Restoration. There will be the usual amount of specialized tastes, curiosity, timidity, laziness, and rattle-brained thinking. The questioning should probe these peculiarities, and stimulate the pupil's ambition to improve his preparation at its weakest point. Needless to say the questions should not be asked with the daily idea of making the pupil fail. Like any other surgical instrument the question probe should be used skillfully and with a proper motive. It would be as great an error to bend your questions continually away from the student's special tastes and abilities as to be perpetually guided by them.

6. The bulk of the teacher's attention should be given neither to the few exceptionally able students nor to the few very poor pupils. It is to the average normal boy and girl that the most of the questioning should be directed. The brilliant student should be called on sufficiently to retain his interest and to set a standard of excellence for the class. He should be given the most difficult of the assignments of outside work and if necessary an additional number of them. As to the few pupils whom the teacher deems exceptionally poor, it may be said that the effect of questioning should never be to discourage the pupil who has made an honest effort at preparation. During the early part of the course the efforts of the teacher may well be directed to asking the backward student

questions to which he can make reasonably satisfactory answers. By saving the student from the daily humiliation of failure before the class, and by tactfully encouraging him to greater effort, the teacher may shortly discover that the poor pupil is far from hopeless.

7. Do not allow your questions to consume a disproportionate amount of time with details. Until very recently in all our history teaching, battles have been exalted to a place immeasurably greater than their importance. We are coming to see that the fighting is one of the least important things in the war. The causes and results, the financial, political, and social effects now absorb our attention. One or two battles in a course may profitably be studied in detail, particularly in the history of our own country, but in the press of considerations far more interesting and vital, it is a waste of time to give more than a moment's notice to the remainder. Student descriptions of battles are bound to be stereotyped. The ordinary textbook describes each of the thousand battles of the world in about the same fifty words.

8. Let some of the questions be directed towards cultivating the student's powers of oral description. History is not altogether a matter of analysis or generalization. There can scarcely be assigned a lesson in history that does not contain events which lend themselves to dramatic description. Their recital should be made the occasion of the student's best efforts in this direction. Let the pupils be

taught to use adjectives and adverbs. Break down the barrier of listlessness or fear or self-consciousness which keeps the student from rendering a graphic and thrilling account of great events.

9. Let the questions from day to day develop the continuity of history. Avoid questioning that fails to unite the events of previous lessons with the one being studied. Bring out the connection of the past and the present. Slavery existed in America for two hundred years before the Civil War was fought. Your teaching of those two centuries of history should be so conducted that when the Civil War is finally reached, the class can tell the process by which anti-slavery sentiment was finally crystallized. The hiatus between the mobbing of Garrison in Boston and the extraordinary contribution of Massachusetts to the Northern army should be bridged, not by a heroic question or two when the war is finally reached, but by a daily attention to the events which effected the metamorphosis.

10. If the answer to your question requires the use of a map, ask it in such a way that the student can talk and use the map at the same time. The geographical provisions of a treaty, the routes of explorers, the grants of commercial companies, campaigns, or military frontiers should all be recited in this way. A wall map with simply the outline of the territory, with its rivers, will be of considerable assistance in testing the accuracy of the student's geographical knowledge. While reciting, let him

locate with chalk or pointer the cities, arbitrary boundary lines, and routes he finds it necessary to mention in his recitation. It will require special attention early in the course to teach students the necessity for preparation of this sort. Like everything else, map work should be reasonable in its requirements. A knowledge of geography is imperative to the correct understanding of history, and the indifference or ignorance of teachers should never excuse inattention to this vital necessity. On the other hand, however, it is equally reprehensible to require of high school students the labored preparation of maps in the drawing of which hours of valuable time are spent in searching for places of trivial importance and small historical value. Map work in a high school history course should require no more than geographical accuracy in locating boundaries, routes, and places really vital to the history of the people being studied. If it does more than this it usurps time disproportionate to its value.

V

VARIOUS MODES OF REVIEW

The place of drill in the history recitation

We have long since learned the folly of spending very many of the minutes of a recitation in drilling students in dates, outlines, and charts. Work of this sort never made a recitation vital; never inspired a student with enthusiasm for historical inquiry; never really dispelled the fog which surrounds, for the student, the cabinets and constitutions, battles and boundaries, declarations and decrees, so briefly treated in the text.

Good reviews will develop a knowledge of the sequence of events

But it may be seriously questioned whether many teachers, in their zeal to escape the over-emphasis of dates, have not gone to the extreme of neglecting them altogether. That a student should remember sufficient dates to fix in his mind the sequence of important events is hardly open to question. That he can never do so without some special attention to dates is equally indisputable. Without doubt, drill in important dates is necessary, but it should be so conducted as to take but little time. Each day the teacher has indicated the dates worthy to be remembered and has been careful to select the landmarks of history. He has called attention to the various collateral circumstances which might assist to fix the dates in the child's mind. The student has kept his list of dates in the back of his text or in some convenient place of reference. Once a week for three minutes the teacher gives the class a rapid review on the dates contained in the list. Occasionally the class are sent to the board and asked to write the dates of the reigns of the English monarchs from William down to the point which the class has reached, or the Presidents in their order, or some other similar exercise calculated to give a backbone to the history being studied. The class will know that such a review is liable to be given at any time. They will endeavor to be prepared. The result will be that with the expenditure of a few minutes at intervals in rapid review, history will cease to be a spineless narrative and become for the student an orderly procession of events. Drill in dates is only one method to this end. There may be a rapid review in battles, generals, wars, treaties, proclamations, and inventions. Such exercises encourage the classification of facts and stimulate fluency of expression. It is of the highest importance for the student so to arrange in his mind what he has learned in recitation that he can call to his command at a second's notice the fact, date, or illustration he desires. There will be many times in his school and college career when such an ability will be indispensable; in business or the professions it is an invaluable asset, infinitely more useful than the history itself. It will be well for the teacher to inquire: "What am I doing to cultivate such an ability in my students?"

They will give a view of the whole subject

Few teachers will deny that too little time is spent in giving the student a general view of the whole subject, either in its entirety or in its various phases. The text has been studied by chapters or by months or by movements. The history as a whole has never been seen. By the time the student has reached the "Aldrich Currency Plan" in American history he has forgotten all about the experiments with the first United States Bank. He could no more outline the financial history of the United States as given in his text than he could outline the industrial or political history of the American people. And yet he has studied the facts given in his textbook; he has supplemented the text by his work in the library, and in the recitation; he has done everything that may reasonably be expected of him, except to assemble his historical information and review it as a whole.

If the student in American history is asked to go to the board at intervals and write an outline for the work covered on such topics as the following, he will come much nearer understanding the progress of our people:—

1. History of the tariff.

2. Political parties and principles for which they stood.

3. Things that crystallized Northern sentiment against slavery.

4.   Reasons for the unification of the South.

5.   Diplomatic relations of the United States.

6.   Additions of territory.

7.   Financial legislation.

8.   Growth of humanitarian spirit.

There will easily be sufficient topics so that each member of the class will have a different one. They can all work at the board, simultaneously. The amount of time used for exercises of this sort need not be great, and the value received is incalculable.

If the teacher wishes to review briefly on the military, diplomatic, social, political, or economic history of the people the class have been studying, it is no difficult matter to arrange a set of questions, the occasional review in which will clinch in the student's mind what otherwise would surely be forgotten. Such questions as the following on the financial history of the United States are each answerable with a few words and will serve as an illustration of the method which may be employed in reviewing any other phase of history:—

1.   By what means was trade accomplished before the use of money?

2.   What are the functions of money?

3.   What determines the amount of money needed in a country?

4. What has been used for money at various periods of our history?

5. What is meant by doing business on credit?

6. What is cheap money?

7. What is Gresham's Law?

8. What is the effect of large issues of paper money on prices?

9. What is the effect of large issues of paper money on wages?

10. Why does the wage-earner suffer?

11. At what periods in American history have large issues of paper money been emitted?

12. What were the objects of the first United States Bank?

13. Did the bank accomplish them?

14. Why was it not rechartered?

15. When was the second United States Bank chartered?

16. Why?

17. What case decided the constitutionality of the bank?

18. Did the second United States Bank accomplish the purpose for which it was formed?

19. Why was the second United States Bank re-chartered?

20. What is meant by "Wildcat Banking"?

21. What are the dates of our greatest panics?

22. What were the chief causes?

23. What was the effect on prices?

24. What on wages?

25. Under what President was the independent treasury first established?

26. Is it in existence to-day?

27. When were greenbacks issued?

28. To what amount?

29. Who was responsible for the issue?

30. Were they legal tender for private debts contracted before their issue?

31. When was the Resumption Act passed?

32. Are the greenbacks in circulation to-day?

33. What is free silver?

34. What was the "Crime of '73"?

35. What was the "Bland-Allison Act"?

36. What was the Currency Act of 1900?

37. What is Bimetallism?

38. What is meant by "Mint Ratio"?

39. What is meant by "Market Ratio"?

40. What is meant by "Free Coinage"?

41. What is meant by "Gratuitous Coinage"?

42. What is meant by "Standard Money"?

43. With the market ratio at 30 to 1 and the mint ratio at 16 to 1, which money would tend to disappear from circulation if both metals are freely coined and made full legal tender?

44. Why is silver not the standard to-day?

45. What is the "Aldrich Plan"?

46. What is a United States bond?

47. Is it a secure investment?

48. What is its average rate of interest?

49. By whom is a national bank chartered?

50. May it issue paper money?

51. When was the first National Banking Act passed?

52. Why?

53. Why should banking business be profitable under the act?

54. What advantage did the Government expect to receive in passing the act?

55. Are deposits guaranteed?

56. May States emit bills of credit?

57. Is it constitutional for banks chartered by the State to emit bills of credit?

58. Do they do so to-day?

59. Why?

Obviously as the year advances, the list of questions for review grows longer. An increasing amount of time should therefore be devoted to work of this sort.

They will insure a better acquaintance with great men and women

The most superficial observation will suffice to convince anyone that high school graduates know very little about the great men and women of history. The character sketches suggested earlier in the chapter, supplemented with occasional reviews, will do much to improve this condition. These drills may be conducted by asking for brief statements on the greatest service or the most distinguishing characteristic of the great men and women met with in the course. The same thing is accomplished by reversing the process and asking such questions as,—"Who was the American Fabius"? or "The Great Compromiser"? or the "Sage of Menlo Park"? etc. Questions on the authorship of great documents, the founders of institutions, the organizers of movements, reformers, philosophers, artists, statesmen, generals, accomplish the same purpose.

They will be economical of time

There are a vast number of review questions answerable with *yes* or *no*. The student's knowledge of the subject may be quickly discovered and a rapid review conducted by a series of such questions. The following list on American history will illustrate the method:—

1. Was Cromwell's colonial policy helpful to the American colonies?

2. Did the Revolution of 1688 have any effect on the colonies?

3. Were the Huguenots excluded from Canada?

4. Were the Writs of Assistance used in England?

5. Did America ever have a theocracy?

6. Did the rule of 1756 affect the people of the colonies?

7. Was the Sugar Act legal?

8. Was there any effort to amend the Articles of Confederation?

9. Does funding a debt lessen it?

10. Did Hamilton's measures tend to centralize power?

11. Did the members of the Constitutional Convention exceed their instructions?

12. Is a cabinet provided for in the Constitution?

13. Does the Constitution of the United States prevent a State from establishing a religion?

14. Is it possible for a State to repudiate its debts?

15. Does the constitutional provision for uniform duties protect the Territories?

16. Was impressment practiced in England?

17. Did the Whigs favor internal improvements?

18. Did the North favor the Force Bill of 1833?

19. Did Massachusetts favor the Tariff of 1816?

20. Did the Republican party stand for the abolition of slavery in 1860?

21. Did the Emancipation Proclamation free all the slaves in the United States?

22. Did the working-men of England favor the South during the Civil War?

23. Was it necessary for the South to resort to the draft?

24. Could a man in 1860 consistently accept both the Dred Scott decision and the doctrine of popular sovereignty?

25. Did Lincoln's assassination have any effect on the reconstruction policy?

26. Does the Federal Constitution compel negro suffrage?

27. Was the Anaconda System successful?

28. Was a President of the United States ever impeached?

29. Were the claims for indirect damages in the Alabama claims allowed?

30. Did Calhoun favor the Compromise of 1850?

31. Did Thaddeus Stevens favor the Fifteenth Amendment to the Constitution?

32. Did Lincoln favor the social equality of the white and black races?

33. Did Grant favor the Tenure of Office Act?

34. Did Lee make more than one attempt to invade the North?

35. Was the "Ohio Idea" ever strong enough to affect legislation?

36. Did Spain have any part in calling out the Monroe Doctrine?

37. Has the United States any control over the debts of Cuba?

38. Has a joint resolution ever been used to acquire territory other than that included in Texas?

39. Has the United States ever resorted to a tax on incomes?

40. Has the Federal Government ever attempted to restrict the power of the press?

41. Is it illegal to-day for a railway to give a cheaper rate to one shipper than to another?

42. Has the Republican party ever reduced the protective tariffs of the war?

43. Did the Civil Service Act passed in 1883 include postmasters?

44. Did the Wilson-Gorman Act reduce the tariff to a revenue basis?

45. Can a railway engaged solely in intra-state business carry a case, involving a reduction of their rates by the State legislature, to the Supreme Court of the United States?

46. Is Utah a part of the Louisiana Purchase?

47. If the mint ratio is 16 to 1 and the market ratio is 17 to 1, will the gold dollar be the standard if there is full legal tender and free coinage for both gold and silver?

48. Is the Canadian frontier fortified?

49. Are the functions of government in this country increasing?

50. Is it possible for a man to be defeated for the Presidency if a majority of the people vote for him?

The great disadvantage of this kind of review is that the students have for their answer a choice between two words, one of which is bound to be correct. Knowing nothing whatever of the subject, they will still stand a fifty per cent chance of answering correctly. The alert teacher should be able to reduce this haphazard answering to a minimum, while still reaping the advantages of rapidity and thoroughness which the plan possesses. Few other methods will cover as much ground in as short time. On the Federal Constitution there are infinite possibilities for "yes and no" questioning, which afford a brief and effective means of review in the principles of American government.

They will secure fluency

Review for the purpose of securing fluency is a consideration frequently lost sight of by high school history teachers. It may be too sanguine to expect fluency of the average student reciting on a topic for the first time. But when it is considered how very many important questions are never recited on but once, the wisdom of an occasional review to secure rapid, fluent, and complete answers to topics previously discussed is readily seen. Select a list of topics that will at one and the same time cultivate fluency and strengthen the memory for the important considerations of history. Fluency in itself does not possess sufficient value to justify the expenditure of recitation time. Facility of expression needs to be cultivated in discussion of the conclusions reached in class which need to be clinched in the student's mind. Such questions as the following will serve as illustrations of the kind adaptable for such purpose, at the middle of a year course in American history:—

1. Give three distinct characteristics of French colonization in America; three of Spanish; three of English.

2. What things did the English colonies possess in common?

3. What were the results to the colonies of the French and Indian War?

4. To what extent was the Revolution brought about by economic causes?

5. What were the defects in the Articles of Confederation?

6. Account for the downfall of the Federalist party.

7. In what ways has democracy advanced since 1789?

8. What were the results of the struggle over the admission of Missouri?

9. Discuss the growth of the sentiment for internal improvements?

10. Describe the social life of the Western pioneer?

What the student may do with 'problems' in history

Still another kind of review of great value in strengthening the student's ability to generalize and analyze, consists of what might be called "problems in history." They are given out in much the same way as original problems in geometry, assuming that the student is acquainted with the facts from which to deduce the answers to the question. The object of such a review is to give the student practice in original thinking. He is not supposed to use a library, but only the facts which are in his text or which have been previously brought out in class recitations.

The following are examples of questions adaptable for this purpose:—

1. Why can the American people be regarded as the world's greatest colonizers?

2. Why could Washington be regarded as only an Englishman living in America?

3. Is it true that the South lost the Civil War because of slavery?

4. In what particulars did Andrew Jackson accurately reflect the spirit or the ideals of the new West?

5.   What is illustrated by the attempt to found the State of Franklin?

6.   What considerations made the secession of the West in our early history a likely possibility?

Questions of this kind, not answered directly in class or in the text, may be given out a day in advance and the answers collected at the next recitation.

VI

THE USE OF WRITTEN REPORTS

The purpose of theme work should change as the course continues

A method frequently employed by teachers of history is to require written reports or themes on various phases of the history as the work progresses. This plan is particularly valuable for the students in the first two years of high school history, for the reason that their library requirements are less exacting and their need of fluency greater during that time than later in their course. The objects of theme work in history courses are usually to arouse the pupil's powers of observation, description, and narration, and to provide means of drill in the exercise of these powers. These should not be the sole purposes of theme work, however. As the year advances, an increasing amount of the written work should be on subjects requiring some generalization or analysis of the facts brought out in the text or in the recitation. The pupil who has written a theme describing the appearance of the Pyramids has completed an exercise in history less valuable than that of the student who writes a theme on the errors of the Athenian Democracy.

To summarize, reviews in history should consist of both oral and written work; they should be rapid enough to insure quick thinking, alert attention, and small expenditure of time; they should occur with increasing frequency as the year advances; they should stock the memory, fix in the student's mind the order of events, stimulate fluency, insure a permanent acquaintance with the personnel of history, and give to the student a better view of the subject as a whole and in its various phases.

VII

EXAMINATIONS AS TESTS OF PROGRESS

*The examination should determine how much the student
has progressed*

The time is coming, if it is not already here, when
the public will cry out against the nervous fear and
sleepless nights with which their children approach
the semi-annual torture of our inquisitorial examinations. That reasonable examinations are essential
and beneficial is hardly open to question. That a student should be expected correctly to answer a fair
percentage of reasonable questions on work which
has been properly taught is not a cause of complaint
from anyone. But that children should be fright-
ened into a state of nervous terror by the bugaboo
of an impending examination, and then be forced
to attempt a series of conundrums propounded by a
teacher who takes pride in maintaining a high percentage of failures, is indefensible. An examination
should not be conducted with the primary object of
making it a thing to be feared. However desirable
such a questionable asset may seem to certain college
professors, it is a serious fault in a high school teacher
to have any considerable number of normal children
fail. The ambition of the good instructor is to give
an examination which shall at once be thorough,
reasonable, and intelligently directed toward finding

what the student has really learned. His purpose is to test accurately the various abilities which he has endeavored to encourage in the student during his course. He wishes to ascertain how much the student has really progressed.

Specific suggestions on formulating questions

In order to do this the examination must be on the really material considerations of the history. Questions on unimportant details should be omitted. The student should not be expected to burden his memory with the limitless mass of petty isolated facts contained in the average history text. The questions should be on considerations that have been carefully discussed, and not on facts that have received but cursory attention.

The examination should not require too much time for writing. The several hours' continuous nervous tension sometimes exacted by too ambitious teachers does the average child more harm than the examination can possibly do him good.

The examination should consist of questions that will jointly or severally test the student's powers of description, generalization, and analysis. They should test his knowledge of the sequence of events, his ability to use a library or a map, his knowledge of the various phases and the various periods of the history studied. In every examination there should be at least one question dealing with the time and the order of events, one each on the geographical, political, and social history, one that is analytical, one that requires generalization, one that will test his knowledge of the library, and one that will test his powers of description. It is not necessary to limit the questions to the customary number of ten. It is frequently advisable to give a class some degree of choice in the selection of their questions by requiring any ten out of a larger number asked. Certainly such a plan gives the student a more favorable opportunity to demonstrate his ability without in the least diminishing the value of the examination.

Examination questions, like all other questions, should be definite, clean-cut, and reasonable. If possible, each student should be supplied with a copy, instead of having the set written on the board. They should cover only those portions of the subject that have been properly taught. The teacher should not expect the boy who has kept no useful notes, whose library work has been haphazard, and whose methods of study have not been supervised, to perform at examination time the miracle of accurately remembering what he has never been properly taught.

Made in the USA
Monee, IL
07 July 2026

56646391R00049